Getting to LONDON

by Rosemary Stones · pictures by Sharon Scotland

Published by Dinosaur Publications

London is the capital city of England. There are so many exciting things to see that this book can only tell you about some of them.

This is Piccadilly Circus in the heart of London. The statue in the middle is of Eros, the god of love.

Eros was the first London sculpture to be made of aluminium. The leg he balances on is solid but the rest of him is hollow. The sculptor was Sir Alfred Gilbert. Eros is the Greek name for the god of love.

Lots of people travel about London on the bus or on the tube. London buses are red and if you go upstairs you will have a good view of the sights.

This is Trafalgar Square where you can feed the pigeons. Some of them are so tame they will perch on your hand or on your head!

Admiralty Arch is the beginning of a very wide road called The Mall which leads to Buckingham Palace.

As you walk down Whitehall you will see the Horseguards on sentry duty. Their horses have been trained to stand still for long periods. On either side of Whitehall are government offices.

Off Whitehall there is a narrow street called Downing Street. 10 Downing Street has always been the home of the Prime Minister. The Chancellor of the Exchequer lives at number 11.

Everyone who works at 10 Downing Street goes in through the famous front door, from typists to the Prime Minister.

At the end of Whitehall is Parliament Square where you can see the Houses of Parliament and Big Ben. Big Ben is a huge clock tower. The clock chimes every quarter of an hour. You will often hear Big Ben chiming on radio and television before news programmes.

The Houses of Parliament are where Members of Parliament from all over the United Kingdom meet to discuss how Britain should be governed. Inside the Houses of Parliament, you will see the House of Commons and the House of Lords where debates take place.

This is Westminster Abbey where the Queen was crowned. The Abbey is nine hundred years old.

When you go inside Westminster Abbey look for the tomb of Queen Elizabeth I and Poets' Corner.

The largest park in London is called Hyde Park. If you go there on a Sunday, you can visit Speaker's Corner where, traditionally, people can make speeches about things that concern them. There is always a big crowd to hear what they have to say.

Do you know about Peter Pan, the boy who lived in Never Never Land and didn't want to grow up? There is a statue of Peter in another famous London park, Kensington Gardens. J. M. Barrie, who wrote *Peter Pan*, put it there secretly at night so that children would think it had arrived by magic.

The Tower of London is a large castle beside the River Thames. In the olden days it had a moat. The oldest part of the Tower of London is the White Tower which was built nine hundred years ago at the time of William the Conqueror. You will see the Crown Jewels, the dungeons where prisoners were once kept and a collection of armour which soldiers wore in battle.

On the lawns of the Tower, are the ravens who always live there. The Tower is guarded by Yeoman Warders or 'Beefeaters' who wear a uniform that is four hundred years old.

From the Tower of London you can see Tower Bridge. When large ships need to pass through the bridge into the Pool of London, the two drawbridges separate and are lifted upwards hydraulically to give the ships headway.

Cars and buses have to wait until the drawbridges are lowered again.

St. Paul's Cathedral was designed by Sir Christopher Wren and finished in 1710. It has an enormous dome. Inside the cathedral you can climb up lots of steps to a gallery in the dome called the Whispering Gallery. If you whisper, the sounds travel round the dome and can be heard by people on the other side.

This is the British Museum, the largest national museum in Britain. It has so many interesting things to see that you could spend weeks here and still miss something. See if you can find the Elgin Marbles, the Magna Carta and the Rosetta Stone.

The Elgin Marbles are part of the Parthenon, a temple in Athens. The Magna Carta is a medieval charter of rights signed by King John. The Rosetta Stone dates back to 196 BC.

At Greenwich Pier you can visit the Cutty Sark, a 19th century tea and wool sailing clipper. A clipper was a very fast sailing ship that carried goods from overseas back to Britain.

A good way to visit Greenwich is to take a boat from Westminster Pier.

Up the hill at Greenwich is the Old Royal Observatory, a small planetarium built for the first astronomer royal in the 17th century. Outside the building you can stand on the Greenwich Meridian – the line which marks Meridian 0.

A meridian is an imaginary line joining the north and south poles at right angles to the equator.

This beautiful palace is Hampton Court. You can reach it by boat just as Henry VIII did. King Henry took Hampton Court from his Lord Chancellor, Wolsey, because he was angry that Wolsey had a finer palace than himself.

The Hampton Court Maze is a giant puzzle – a network of connecting paths separated by thick hedges. It is fun to get lost there.

The maze was probably planted in the reign of Queen Anne, the last of the Stuart monarchs.

Battersea Power station with its four giant chimneys used to make power for a large area of London. It was built 50 years ago and it shows that even industrial buildings can be striking and beautiful to look at.

Battersea Power station is being turned into a leisure complex.